This Book Belongs To

_____

_____

my real story

ONE YEAR *to* RECORD, REFLECT, *and* REMEMBER

Becky Thompson

WATERBROOK

MY REAL STORY

Trade Paperback ISBN 978-0-525-65251-9

Published in the United States by WaterBrook, an imprint of the Crown Publishing Group, a division of Penguin Random House LLC, New York.

WATERBROOK® and its deer colophon are registered trademarks of Penguin Random House LLC.

Printed in China
2019—First Edition

10 9 8 7 6 5 4 3 2 1

SPECIAL SALES
Most WaterBrook books are available at special quantity discounts when purchased in bulk by corporations, organizations, and special-interest groups. Custom imprinting or excerpting can also be done to fit special needs. For information, please email specialmarketscms@penguinrandomhouse.com or call 1-800-603-7051.

Introduction

I t was windy that night. I'm not sure how windy; Scripture doesn't say. It just says the boat was already some distance from land, battered by the waves because the wind was against it.

You know this story from Matthew 14:22–33. It's the one where Jesus (and Peter) walked on water. Jesus's disciples were in a boat crossing to the other side of the lake when Jesus caught up to them by walking on the water.

At first His friends thought He was a ghost, but when Jesus called out to them, Peter recognized His voice and answered, "Lord, if it's you, tell me to come to you on the water."

"Come," Jesus answered.

And Peter climbed out of the boat and began walking to Jesus.

Peter was okay until he took his eyes off the Lord, noticed the waves, and began to sink. Desperate, Peter cried out, "Lord! Save me!"

Scripture says that Jesus reached out and caught him.

Have you ever really considered what it must have been like to be standing next to Jesus one moment and neck deep in water the next? (Maybe you feel like that now.) I wish Scripture were clearer about what happened next. But this is what I imagine took place. I don't think Jesus and Peter swam back to the boat. I don't think Jesus walked on the water while dragging Peter by his arm. Can you even imagine how ridiculous that would have been?

Instead, I think Jesus lifted Peter up out of the water and they walked back to the boat together. I think Peter climbed into the boat wet ... and I believe he never forgot the importance of having someone reach down and pull him up.

Sometime later—after Jesus went to heaven—Peter and John went to the temple to pray. Scripture says,

> As they approached the Temple, a man lame from birth was being carried in.... When he saw Peter and John about to enter, he asked them for some money.
>
> Peter and John looked at him intently, and Peter said, "Look at us!" The lame man looked at them eagerly, expecting some money. But Peter said, "I don't have any silver or gold for you. But I'll give you what I have. In the name of Jesus Christ the Nazarene, get up and walk!"
>
> Then Peter took the lame man by the right hand and helped him up. And as he did, the man's feet and ankles were instantly healed and strengthened. He jumped up, stood on his feet, and began to walk! Then, walking, leaping, and praising God, he went into the Temple with them. (Acts 3:2–8, NLT)

I wonder if Peter remembered that night in the water with Jesus as he stood over the crippled man. I wonder if he thought of how Jesus had stood over him in the same way. I wonder if he saw himself in the face of that man. And I wonder if the moment Peter reached down and extended his arm to lift him to his feet, he felt the power of God moving through his hand the same way Jesus did when lifting Peter.

There is something powerful that happens when you encounter God in a certain way, when you have the opportunity to experience Jesus as the One who will stand over you and pull you from the water that tries to drown you. In that moment you learn how to do something you wouldn't otherwise know. You learn how to pull others to their feet and navigate them through troubled waters.

When Peter was sinking, he didn't shout, "This is going to make a great story someday!" He just shouted, "Lord, save me!" Yet Peter's story is told over and over again to teach us, inspire us, and help us to better understand our Lord.

So here's my question: What if we were able to recognize the story that God was writing in our lives as we were living it? When life is difficult and we are struggling, we usually don't think about the people we will be able to help through the story of how God rescued us. It can be hard to remember that there is purpose woven throughout every moment of our lives. Not just purpose for us but purpose for others as well. What thoughts or memories or circumstances would you record if you knew that someday someone was going to need to hear how God brought you through this time? What would you want to document? What would you want to remember? What would you want to say to someone who is about to walk through a similar season or situation?

What is the real story of this season?

Your answers to the questions on the pages ahead will be unique to you. They likely will be different in this season than they would have been in seasons past or would be in those to come. Your story is continuously being written, so it's important that you document it. Recording and then revisiting *your real story* will remind you of what God has done. It will open your eyes to what He is currently doing, and it will prepare you to share with others what He can do for them.

You have lived a story. You *are* living a story. And you have a story to tell. Take notes, friend.

We all have stories. This is yours.

With love,

Becky

my story

Every story has a beginning. Your story was being written long before you were born. A million small moments and decisions all led to the creation of you. And before anyone on earth knew you were coming, God saw you and knew you intimately. He saw every second that built up to the moment you would come to meet Him for the first time. Can you imagine His joy as you traveled down the path that led you to Him?

WHERE WERE YOU AND WHAT WAS HAPPENING
WHEN YOU DECIDED TO FOLLOW JESUS AND
MAKE HIM THE LORD OF YOUR LIFE?

to be honest...

THIS IS HOW I REALLY FEEL TODAY

Lord, just as You saw the beginning of my story, You see me right here ... right now. Sometimes I forget that You don't show up just for the important moments in my life but that You walk every step with me. I want to pause right now and declare that I trust You with every detail of my story. Thank You for remaining with me always and continuing to lead my heart with Your love. In Jesus's name, amen.

for the record

THESE ARE THE MOMENTS I DON'T WANT TO FORGET

give thanks

in all circumstances

3 THINGS I'M THANKFUL FOR TODAY

1

2

3

my story

I sat awestruck in my high school youth group as I listened to a man tell about his dark past and how God had radically saved him. I thought of my own life. It didn't seem nearly as interesting, and I wondered what story I had to tell. The truth is, God finds some of us in addiction or rebellion, others in pain and despair, and others who are happy and going through ordinary circumstances. No matter what our lives were like before we gave Him our hearts, it is always a miracle when we say yes to following the Lord.

WHEN YOU GAVE YOUR LIFE TO THE LORD,
WHAT DID GOD RESCUE YOU FROM?

to be honest ...

THIS IS HOW I REALLY FEEL TODAY

Lord, You are continually rescuing me from the plots and plans of the Enemy. Even when I am unaware that You are moving in my behalf, You fight for me. Thank You for rescuing me from my own foolishness and from the one who would seek to destroy me in any way he can. Help me remember to praise You for always being my deliverer. In Jesus's name, amen.

for the record

THESE ARE THE MOMENTS I DON'T WANT TO FORGET

give thanks

in all circumstances

---

3 THINGS I'M THANKFUL FOR TODAY

1

2

3

my story

Everyone else was asleep as I sat on the top bunk of my sons' bed and talked quietly with my oldest. I was reminding him of God's love for him while retelling the gospel story. My son had already invited Jesus to be the Lord of his life, but something clicked as I painted a picture of our loving Savior in a new way. Suddenly, overwhelmed with emotion, my son began to sob, saying, "God is real and He loves me." We all have different responses when the Lord becomes deeply real to us.

WHEN GOD BECAME REAL TO YOU,
HOW DID YOU RESPOND?

to be honest...

THIS IS HOW I REALLY FEEL TODAY

Lord, I want my heart to continue to burn with love and passion for You. I don't want my love for You to become routine or forced. And I certainly don't want to become so unmoved by the truth of Your redeeming love that I take it for granted. Because I know Your love for me never changes, help me love You in response. Fan the fire of my love for You within me as You remind me of all You have done. In Jesus's name, amen.

for the record

THESE ARE THE MOMENTS I DON'T WANT TO FORGET

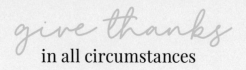

give thanks

in all circumstances

3 THINGS I'M THANKFUL FOR TODAY

1

2

3

my story

When I was young, I had a Sunday school teacher who mailed handwritten postcards to each child in her class every week. Halfway to Sunday, her note would arrive and remind me of the previous week's lesson. She always expressed interest in something that mattered to me and never failed to conclude with "Jesus loves you and so do I." That kind woman made such an impact on my early walk with the Lord, revealing God's compassionate and intentional love. We all have people in our lives who put God's love on display for us to see and experience.

WHO WERE SOME OF THE FIRST PEOPLE TO REVEAL GOD'S CHARACTER TO YOU THROUGH THEIR ACTIONS?

to be honest ...

THIS IS HOW I REALLY FEEL TODAY

Lord, in Your Word You commanded us to love You with all our hearts and also to love our neighbors as much as we love ourselves. I don't want to forget that both are equally important to You. In order to follow You, I need to love those around me as much as I love You. Show me opportunities to love others well this week. In Jesus's name, amen.

for the record

THESE ARE THE MOMENTS I DON'T WANT TO FORGET

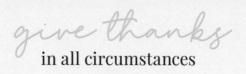

in all circumstances

3 THINGS I'M THANKFUL FOR TODAY

1

2

3

my story

A relationship with Jesus does not guarantee that life will be easy and free from pain. It does mean, however, that Jesus will be with us through every hardship and trial. I'm always encouraged when I read Jesus's words in Luke 22:31–32: "Simon, Simon, Satan has asked to sift you as wheat. But I have prayed for you, Simon, that your faith may not fail." In this scripture, Jesus reveals to us that Christians are not free from the attacks of our enemy, but we don't face them alone. Jesus is with us and intercedes for us, strengthening us and our faith in Him.

WHAT WAS ONE OF THE MOST FAITH-TESTING TRIALS YOU FACED IN YOUR EARLY WALK WITH THE LORD?

to be honest...

THIS IS HOW I REALLY FEEL TODAY

Lord, whatever might come against me, I can rest knowing that I am cared for by the God who is Lord over all and who sends me help in my times of need. Through the sacrifice of Jesus I have direct access to You, and in the Holy Spirit I have a constant guide. Help me cling to this hope in the week ahead. In Jesus's name, amen.

DATE

for the record

THESE ARE THE MOMENTS I DON'T WANT TO FORGET

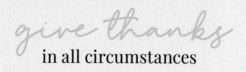
give thanks
in all circumstances

———————

3 THINGS I'M THANKFUL FOR TODAY

DATE

1

2

3

my story

When my family and I moved across the country last year, I discovered that the life experiences of my neighbors were as different as the landscape. I missed being around people who understood the lens through which I viewed the world, who knew what it felt like to be me. I craved a tribe of like-hearted friends. When we become followers of Jesus, we long to interact with people on a similar faith journey.

WHEN YOU FIRST CAME INTO A RELATIONSHIP WITH THE LORD, WHO WERE THE PEOPLE WHO WALKED CLOSELY ALONGSIDE YOU?

to be honest...

THIS IS HOW I REALLY FEEL TODAY

Lord, You know my need for fellowship with others on a similar journey. You know how much I need to be in relationship with people who believe and feel as I do. Thank You for caring about community, and thank You for bringing people into my life whom I can share with and walk shoulder to shoulder with as I follow You. In Jesus's name, amen.

for the record

THESE ARE THE MOMENTS I DON'T WANT TO FORGET

give thanks

in all circumstances

3 THINGS I'M THANKFUL FOR TODAY

1

2

3

my story

My husband and I met when we were both young. I was just nineteen and he was twenty-three when we said our vows. In those early days, we tried to spend all our time together. We never wanted to be apart. If we're honest, most of us felt that way about the Lord when we first came into a relationship with Him. Whether it was a devotion to prayer, dedicated time reading the Word, or a commitment to attend church weekly, we just wanted more time in His presence.

<<<<<

DESCRIBE HOW TIME SPENT WITH
THE LORD LOOKED WHEN YOU FIRST
GAVE YOUR HEART TO HIM.

>>>>>

to be honest ...

THIS IS HOW I REALLY FEEL TODAY

Lord, I confess that I'm easily distracted. While I desire to focus on You, I am often consumed by my own thoughts, worries, and selfish ambitions. I know You love me. Help me remember that if I'm going to hear Your voice clearly and follow You well, I need to spend time tuning my heart to what You have to say. Help me find time to spend with You this week. In Jesus's name, amen.

for the record

THESE ARE THE MOMENTS I DON'T WANT TO FORGET

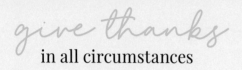

in all circumstances

---

3 THINGS I'M THANKFUL FOR TODAY

1

2

3

my story

There is a story found in Genesis 16 about a pregnant servant woman named Hagar. Hagar was mistreated by her mistress and fled to the desert. She was alone, afraid, and without much hope for her future. But the Lord spoke hope to Hagar's heart, and she responded, "You are the God who sees me." Even in our suffering, even in our pain, just when we are fully convinced we are all alone, God meets us and we become aware of His presence.

WHERE WERE YOU AND WHAT WAS
HAPPENING THE FIRST TIME YOU WERE
SURE THAT THE LORD WAS WITH YOU?

to be honest...

THIS IS HOW I REALLY FEEL TODAY

Lord, when You come into the room, You bring all of who You are. You don't leave Your kindness in heaven or Your gentleness somewhere else. You bring every part of You when You come. I love Your presence because I discover new aspects of Your character when You are with me. Help me be aware of Your steadfast love that never leaves me. Help me look for You throughout my week. In Jesus's name, amen.

for the record

THESE ARE THE MOMENTS I DON'T WANT TO FORGET

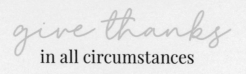

in all circumstances

---

3 THINGS I'M THANKFUL FOR TODAY

DATE

1

2

3

my story

I *can't do that!* I remember protesting, begging the Lord to ask me to do anything but pray for the woman in the hallway. I was sure God had asked me to stop as I rushed to my next college class, but I wanted to pretend He hadn't. The truth is, the Lord is constantly inviting us to be a part of the stories He is writing in the lives of those around us. Yet many of us rush right by, afraid to step outside our comfort zones.

WHAT IS THE MOST INTIMIDATING
THING THE LORD HAS ASKED YOU TO DO
SINCE YOU BECAME A BELIEVER?

to be honest ...

THIS IS HOW I REALLY FEEL TODAY

Lord, when I hear about people who have stepped outside their comfort zones and followed You, I become inspired. Stories such as these ignite fresh passion in my heart to do whatever it is You have asked me to do. I want to be used by You. Lord, give me opportunities to live a bold life of adventure. Give me opportunities to live out stories that will inspire others. I ask for the chance to be used by You to influence the lives of those around me. In Jesus's name, amen.

DATE

for the record

THESE ARE THE MOMENTS I DON'T WANT TO FORGET

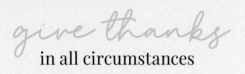

in all circumstances

3 THINGS I'M THANKFUL FOR TODAY

1

2

3

my story

S ongs can be powerful. They can communi-
cate what we are unable to express in our
own words. There are certain worship songs
that remind me of different trials the Lord has
brought me through in the past. In college, one
particular song became an anthem of God's
faithfulness even when I felt unsure. When I
became a new bride, another song reminded
me of God's perfect guidance and the love my
husband and I shared. What song would you
identify as the anthem of this season if it came
on the radio five years from now?

IS THERE A PARTICULAR SONG THAT GOD
USES TO ENCOURAGE YOUR HEART IN THIS
SEASON? WHY IS IT SO MEANINGFUL?

to be honest...

THIS IS HOW I REALLY FEEL TODAY

Lord, one of the most powerful weapons You have given me is the ability to praise You in all circumstances. As I lift my heart and worship You, the Enemy flees. Father, help me remember that the strength to face whatever comes my way is found in praising Your name. In Jesus's name, amen.

for the record

THESE ARE THE MOMENTS I DON'T WANT TO FORGET

give thanks

in all circumstances

3 THINGS I'M THANKFUL FOR TODAY

1

2

3

my story

One afternoon during my freshman year of college, I felt particularly discouraged. I had had a fight with my roommate, I had a big project due, and the guy I liked seemed to be stringing me along. As I walked back to my dorm after class, wondering if God even understood how I felt, I found a small card on the ground that read, "Smile, Becky, Jesus loves you." I assumed someone had dropped it and it was likely meant for another Becky, but that didn't matter. I knew God had put it there just for me.

WHAT HAS GOD DONE RECENTLY TO MAKE
SURE YOU KNOW YOU'RE LOVED AND SEEN?

to be honest...

THIS IS HOW I REALLY FEEL TODAY

Lord, I know You see me. I know You are always there, but at times I can't feel Your presence. I ask that You would reveal Yourself this week. I ask that You would send people into my life to remind me that You're near. My heart longs to be confident in Your unfailing love. Secure my heart in this truth this week. In Jesus's name, amen.

for the record

THESE ARE THE MOMENTS I DON'T WANT TO FORGET

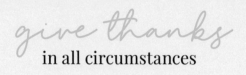

in all circumstances

---

3 THINGS I'M THANKFUL FOR TODAY

DATE

1

2

3

my story

Have you ever been in the middle of a very complicated situation and wondered, *God, how are You going to lead me out of this one?* Often, from our perspective, we see limited options. We believe God can do either A or B. But our God is the God of miracles. He can create infinite possibilities and make a way where there is no other way. We just might not be able to see a good outcome from where we are standing today.

≪≪≪≪≪

WHAT OBSTACLE ARE YOU MOST CURIOUS TO SEE GOD WORK OUT IN THIS SEASON?

≫≫≫≫≫

to be honest ...

THIS IS HOW I REALLY FEEL TODAY

Lord, thank You for the work You are doing behind the scenes. Sometimes I forget there is more going on than what I can see. So, Father, I pray as Jesus taught us to pray, "Your Kingdom come, Your will be done on earth as it is in heaven," in my life, in my family, and in my community. Your heart for me is kind, and Your plans for me are good. In Jesus's name, amen.

for the record

THESE ARE THE MOMENTS I DON'T WANT TO FORGET

give thanks
in all circumstances

3 THINGS I'M THANKFUL FOR TODAY

1

2

3

my story

God connects us to people throughout our lives for many reasons. Right now, if I need to be reminded that God knows what He's doing in my life, I call a certain friend. If I want to laugh about some of the most ridiculous parts of motherhood, I text another friend. These women have not always been in my life, but the Lord knew I would need them right now. My mom always says, "Some people come into our lives for a reason. Some come for a season. And some people come and stay."

WHO HAS GOD BROUGHT INTO YOUR LIFE IN THIS SEASON?

to be honest ...

THIS IS HOW I REALLY FEEL TODAY

Lord, my heart longs to be in deep relationship with others. Though some people need a large community and others need just a few close friends, I believe we all desire to know people we can count on and who can count on us. Thank You, God, for the people You've brought into my life in this season. Help me become the type of friend I'd like to have. In Jesus's name, amen.

for the record

THESE ARE THE MOMENTS I DON'T WANT TO FORGET

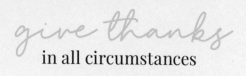
give thanks

in all circumstances

3 THINGS I'M THANKFUL FOR TODAY

DATE

1

2

3

my story

I stayed up late researching all my options. If I was going to become a successful wedding photographer, I needed to learn the latest trends and tricks of the trade. In that season, as I worked to build my business, I prayed that the Lord would open doors. I prayed for wisdom. I prayed for opportunity. Ten years later, I'm no longer a full-time photographer. That season has come and gone. Now I pray for the Lord's help and guidance in other areas of my life. Our prayers say a lot about what matters most to us in each season.

WHAT DO YOU PRAY FOR CONTINUALLY IN THIS SEASON?

to be honest ...

THIS IS HOW I REALLY FEEL TODAY

Lord, You know the deep desires of my heart because You placed them there. You are the One who causes me to dream for Your kingdom and the role I might play in helping it grow. Right now, I ask You to give me the desires of Your heart. If I need to expand my dreams or exchange what I've been holding on to for what You have instead, I am willing. Kindly place Your dreams within me for the seasons ahead. In Jesus's name, amen.

for the record

THESE ARE THE MOMENTS I DON'T WANT TO FORGET

give thanks
in all circumstances

3 THINGS I'M THANKFUL FOR TODAY

1

2

3

my story

Philippians 4:6 reminds us not to be anxious for anything. While this is solid biblical instruction, we can't guarantee that anxiety won't come. The question is, When stress and anxiety try to steal our peace, what do we do? How do we handle these feelings? Prayer is our first line of defense against all fear, but in addition to prayer, we all deal with stress and anxiety in our own way. Some might take a walk. Others might call a friend. Some of us might take on a creative project or simply give ourselves permission to rest for a while.

WHAT DO YOU DO WHEN YOU FEEL ANXIOUS OR STRESSED?

to be honest...

THIS IS HOW I REALLY FEEL TODAY

Lord, all fear must bow in Your presence. When fear and anxiety attempt to overtake my heart, I often fail to praise You and let You go to battle for me. If anxiety tries to steal my peace this week, I ask that You'd quickly prompt me to enter into a posture of praise rather than shrink back in silence. In Jesus's name, amen.

for the record

THESE ARE THE MOMENTS I DON'T WANT TO FORGET

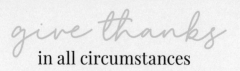

in all circumstances

———

3 THINGS I'M THANKFUL FOR TODAY

1

2

3

my story

There have been many times in my life when I couldn't see much beyond where I stood. I couldn't see what God had planned. I trusted the Lord to lead me as He knew best, yet my heart longed to know where He was taking me. An important biblical principle can be found in our desire to see and follow God's heart for our future. Proverbs 29:18 says, "Where there is no vision, the people perish" (KJV). Sometimes we can't see exactly what lies ahead, but if we can imagine in our hearts a future where God is with us and can trust that He has our best interests at heart, then we will have all we need.

WHAT IS YOUR BIGGEST HOPE FOR TOMORROW?

to be honest...

THIS IS HOW I REALLY FEEL TODAY

Lord, stir hope within me. One of the Enemy's favorite strategies is to drop a lie into my mind that says, "It will always be this way." I respond by calling that exactly what it is: an assault against the truth that You, God, are constantly intervening and forever working miracles in my behalf. I am not stuck. I am not trapped. I am not bound to the belief that life can be only what it is today. Give me hope for tomorrow. In Jesus's name, amen.

for the record

THESE ARE THE MOMENTS I DON'T WANT TO FORGET

give thanks
in all circumstances

3 THINGS I'M THANKFUL FOR TODAY

1

2

3

my story

"What am I being called to do for God in this season? Everything just feels so ordinary," my friend said. Though she was a fantastic wife and mother, I could absolutely relate to her thoughts. I've experienced seasons of my marriage, motherhood, and work life that have felt ordinary and unimportant. While I recognize these assignments are a huge privilege, going through the motions has at times stolen my gratitude. I haven't been able to see the blessings of the season because it's easier to see the daily demands. We often overlook the importance of what we are doing for the Lord.

‹‹‹‹‹

WHAT IS THE MOST REMARKABLE THING GOD HAS ASKED YOU TO DO IN THIS SEASON?

››››››

to be honest...

THIS IS HOW I REALLY FEEL TODAY

Lord, if I'm honest, I sometimes don't appreciate what You have given me to do, because it feels more like an assignment that has to be completed than an adventure I get to take with You. Give me a fresh outlook for these days, God. Help me notice every incredible opportunity I have right now to further Your kingdom. In Jesus's name, amen.

for the record

THESE ARE THE MOMENTS I DON'T WANT TO FORGET

give thanks
in all circumstances

---

3 THINGS I'M THANKFUL FOR TODAY

1

2

3

my story

I f I just had more... Have you ever thought that? If I just had more time, I would absolutely say yes to helping with that ministry. If I just had more money, I'd support that work financially. Often we feel as though time and money are prerequisites for growing God's kingdom, when in reality God can use the least amount of both. He's the God who takes what we have and multiplies it. If you're curious about where you should start serving or what God is calling you to do, answer this week's question.

<<<<<

IF TIME AND MONEY WERE NOT AN ISSUE,
WHAT WOULD YOU DO FOR THE KINGDOM?

>>>>>

to be honest ...

THIS IS HOW I REALLY FEEL TODAY

Lord, I want to be all-in, giving my whole heart and life to the service of Your kingdom. But the reality is that my limited time and money sometimes seem to stand in the way of what I am able to do for You. Teach me how to dream with You, Lord. Teach me how to think and imagine and believe that You are going to make a way for me to partner with You in spreading the message of the gospel. In Jesus's name, amen.

for the record

THESE ARE THE MOMENTS I DON'T WANT TO FORGET

give thanks
in all circumstances

3 THINGS I'M THANKFUL FOR TODAY

1

2

3

my story

Do you ever disqualify yourself from being an encouragement to others because you need some help feeling encouraged yourself? Maybe you feel overwhelmed in your marriage, so you aren't sure you can help a friend struggling in hers. Maybe you are barely keeping it together as a mom, so you don't know how to reach out to another mom who feels as though she's sinking too. The truth is, you don't need to have it all together for God to use you to bring hope or healing to others. You are uniquely positioned to help someone right now.

WHOM CAN YOU ENCOURAGE OR REACH
WITH GOD'S LOVE IN THIS SEASON?

to be honest ...

THIS IS HOW I REALLY FEEL TODAY

Lord, I get so focused on what I need that I often forget I can help others. I expend energy wishing someone would come alongside me instead of recognizing the opportunities You create for me to support another. I just might be the answer to someone else's prayer. Help me look for people to encourage or reach with Your love right now. In Jesus's name, amen.

for the record

THESE ARE THE MOMENTS I DON'T WANT TO FORGET

give thanks

in all circumstances

3 THINGS I'M THANKFUL FOR TODAY

1

2

3

my story

Growing up, I lived on a street with many other little girls my age. We played together every day, running between houses and enjoying our quiet neighborhood. One by one my friends moved away, and eventually I moved as well. It was strange to transition from constant community to occasional get-togethers. The communities God calls us into shift and change with the seasons we are in. Sometimes we are surrounded by like-hearted people, and other times we have to be intentional about building community.

WHAT HAS THE EVOLUTION OF COMMUNITY BEEN LIKE IN YOUR LIFE OVER THE LAST FIVE YEARS? IN WHICH SEASON HAVE YOU THRIVED THE MOST?

to be honest...

THIS IS HOW I REALLY FEEL TODAY

Lord, thank You for the people You have sent into my life when I needed them most. Thank You for the ones I have known for ages and for the ones I knew for only a short time. I ask that You would bless the people who have been a part of my story. You know each one. Continue to guide them in Your love and provide for them in every area of their lives. In Jesus's name, amen.

for the record

THESE ARE THE MOMENTS I DON'T WANT TO FORGET

give thanks
in all circumstances

---

3 THINGS I'M THANKFUL FOR TODAY

1

2

3

my story

Even when all is well, a few challenges usually remain in the background of my heart, stealing some of my peace and joy. As I rinse dishes or fold clothes or drive down the road, my mind wanders to those pressing problems. Sometimes they are personal, and other times they are issues in my community. The Lord reminds us to bring our petitions to Him with gratitude because He carries the weight of anything that tries to hinder our hope.

WHAT ARE THE ISSUES THAT WEIGH
HEAVIEST ON YOUR HEART RIGHT NOW?

to be honest ...

THIS IS HOW I REALLY FEEL TODAY

Lord, some things I can't change. These are the areas that reveal just how much I need You. My only option is prayer. So I pause and bring these situations before You. Thank You for Your care and provision. You can change anything in an instant. Though these worries weigh heavily on my heart, I have full confidence in You as I remember that You're not worried at all. Give me Your peace as I continue to pray. In Jesus's name, amen.

for the record

THESE ARE THE MOMENTS I DON'T WANT TO FORGET

give thanks
in all circumstances

---

3 THINGS I'M THANKFUL FOR TODAY

1

2

3

my story

Even though the storms rage, God will save you. Even though it looks hopeless, God will come through. Even though you feel alone, God will comfort you with His presence. Even though there seems to be no way out, God has already prepared the road ahead. Even though the battle is relentless, God will be your shield. Even though you feel like a failure, God will remind you of your worth and success in Him. In every season, God is faithful.

FILL IN THESE BLANKS:

EVEN THOUGH _____, I KNOW

THAT GOD WILL _____.

to be honest ...

THIS IS HOW I REALLY FEEL TODAY

Lord, I choose today to stand on Your promises. I choose today to believe Your Word. While sometimes my thoughts don't agree with what I read in the Bible, I choose to believe what You say instead of what I think. I will remember that You are faithful, loving, and kind. Today I commit to combatting every fear and emotion that tries to exalt itself above You. In Jesus's name, amen.

for the record

THESE ARE THE MOMENTS I DON'T WANT TO FORGET

give thanks
in all circumstances

---

3 THINGS I'M THANKFUL FOR TODAY

1

2

3

my story

After my freshman year of college, I got a job where I could sit and read while I waited for customers to arrive. I would spend hours every day reading my Bible and journaling. It was a very unique season. Today, with a busier schedule and far less free time, my quiet time looks much different. The best news is that God uses every moment we spend in His presence to refine and revive our hearts (even when we don't have many to offer).

WHAT DOES YOUR PRAYER LIFE/WORSHIP TIME/DEVOTION TIME CURRENTLY LOOK LIKE?

to be honest...

THIS IS HOW I REALLY FEEL TODAY

Lord, You are the God who multiplies. You multiplied the small boy's bread and fish to feed a crowd. You multiply my faith when I struggle with unbelief. You multiply the weary mom's rest so she can care for her children. You multiply everything Your children offer to You. Father, I ask that You would take the time I spend in Your presence and multiply the impact of those moments throughout the day. In Jesus's name, amen.

for the record

THESE ARE THE MOMENTS I DON'T WANT TO FORGET

give thanks
in all circumstances

3 THINGS I'M THANKFUL FOR TODAY

1

2

3

my story

Have you ever gone through something and wished you could tell others what you were really experiencing? Maybe you kept it to yourself so you wouldn't be embarrassed. Maybe you felt ashamed. Maybe you just didn't trust others to keep your personal business to themselves. Or perhaps you didn't know how another person would respond if you were to open your heart and share the truth. Life can feel isolating when we keep our deepest feelings to ourselves. Yet Galatians 6:2 reminds us to "carry each other's burdens."

WHAT DO YOU WISH YOU COULD BE MORE HONEST
WITH OTHERS ABOUT IN THIS SEASON OF LIFE?

to be honest ...

THIS IS HOW I REALLY FEEL TODAY

Lord, give me opportunities to share my true heart with others. Bring people into my life whom I can trust. I know I cannot carry the weight of what's really going on alone. Please increase my boldness to be honest with others. Your Word reminds Your people to look after one another. Give me the courage to share so I can move through this season without becoming weighed down or stuck. In Jesus's name, amen.

for the record

DATE

THESE ARE THE MOMENTS I DON'T WANT TO FORGET

give thanks
in all circumstances

---

3 THINGS I'M THANKFUL FOR TODAY

1

2

3

my story

The Bible tells the story of God's relentless pursuit of relationship with His creation—us. Throughout the Word, this story unfolds as God shows up in the lives of His people in unexpected places. God met one man as he fled from his brother (Genesis 28:10–22). Jesus met a woman beside a well (John 4:1–26), and He met a mother whose son had just died (Luke 7:11–17). He talked with men and women as He traveled. God showed up again and again at just the right time to change lives, prove His love, and expand His kingdom.

IN THIS SEASON, WHERE DO YOU
FIND GOD MEETING YOU?

to be honest ...

THIS IS HOW I REALLY FEEL TODAY

Lord, thank You for being the God who shows up in the middle of my day. You don't wait until I have time set aside; You just meet me right where I am. I ask that You would open my eyes to Your presence today. I ask that You would draw my heart away with You even while I am in the middle of everything else. Remind me that You are good, that You are real, and that You love me. In Jesus's name, amen.

for the record

THESE ARE THE MOMENTS I DON'T WANT TO FORGET

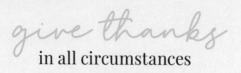

in all circumstances

---

3 THINGS I'M THANKFUL FOR TODAY

1

2

3

my story

Scripture reminds us, "God demonstrates his own love for us in this: While we were still sinners, Christ died for us" (Romans 5:8). We believe deeply that God loves us, because He sent Jesus to rescue us from a life spent apart from Him, yet God confirms His love in many other ways. The blessings God gives us because we are His sons and daughters all testify to His great love for us. In each season we can experience His love in a new way.

←←←←←

WHAT CAUSES YOU TO SAY, "GOD MUST REALLY LOVE ME"?

→→→→→

to be honest...

THIS IS HOW I REALLY FEEL TODAY

Lord, You revealed Your love when You pulled off Your crazy rescue plan and sent Your Son to die for us. You revealed Your love again when You sent Your Holy Spirit to remain with us as a constant comforter and guide. Yet I often become fixated on my flaws and believe there are parts of me that would cause You to withhold Your love from me. Re-center my heart on the truth that I am loved beyond measure. In Jesus's name, amen.

for the record

THESE ARE THE MOMENTS I DON'T WANT TO FORGET

give thanks
in all circumstances

3 THINGS I'M THANKFUL FOR TODAY

1

2

3

my story

No matter how we plan for our future, the Lord leads us in His perfect love. It's comforting to know we have a God who knows what's coming and carefully guides us, asking us to trust Him along the way. Still, sometimes His plans don't exactly match our own. Other times we arrive precisely where we expected, yet it doesn't feel quite as we imagined it would. Whether our circumstances or our emotions are different than we anticipated, each season has its own surprises.

WHAT HAS BEEN THE MOST SURPRISING
PART OF THE LAST SIX MONTHS OF LIFE?

to be honest ...

THIS IS HOW I REALLY FEEL TODAY

Lord, if I could see what You see, I would never be surprised, but an important part of life is trusting Your vision. You're never surprised, God. Circumstances and situations don't sneak up on You. Give me the faith to trust You as You lead me. Give me the grace to remember that while I will certainly face the unexpected, You already factored these outcomes into Your plans for me. In Jesus's name, amen.

for the record

THESE ARE THE MOMENTS I DON'T WANT TO FORGET

give thanks
in all circumstances

3 THINGS I'M THANKFUL FOR TODAY

DATE

1

2

3

my story

L ife can be tricky. I find that some of my most joyful moments are tangled up with the difficult ones. Have you ever noticed this to be true? Personally, I enjoy time with like-hearted friends. I know the Lord uses these moments to refresh my heart so I can better love my family and give my all to my other tasks and responsibilities. However, relationships can also bring misunderstandings and other complications. These difficulties provide opportunities for God to work in our lives.

WHAT ARE SOME OF THE AREAS IN YOUR LIFE RIGHT NOW WHERE JOY AND FRUSTRATION SEEM TO BE INTERTWINED?

to be honest ...

THIS IS HOW I REALLY FEEL TODAY

Lord, I ask that Your will would be done in every area of my life. God, when I want to pull back from circumstances that feel too hard or uncomfortable, help me engage them with grace and love. May Your desires for me and others be fulfilled even in conflict and tangled areas of life. Give me the courage to love others well even when things become complicated. In Jesus's name, amen.

for the record

THESE ARE THE MOMENTS I DON'T WANT TO FORGET

give thanks
in all circumstances

---

3 THINGS I'M THANKFUL FOR TODAY

1

2

3

my story

Have you ever been in the middle of a season that felt ridiculously routine? Maybe your days all blurred together with no end in sight and you struggled to find hope that tomorrow might be different. It could have been a financially difficult time or an emotionally exhausting period. When you're ready to move from one season to the next, it's common to look for signposts or indications that your circumstances are shifting. What have been the major signposts of this season?

HOW IS GOD ENCOURAGING YOUR HEART
TO BELIEVE THAT LIFE WON'T ALWAYS
BE JUST THE WAY IT IS RIGHT NOW?

to be honest...

THIS IS HOW I REALLY FEEL TODAY

Lord, just like the weather turns cooler and the trees begin to change, showing us that the next season will soon arrive, You mark the changing of seasons in our lives as well. Your Holy Spirit moves in my heart like wind, and I sense that something different is about to take place. Help me recognize the shifting of the seasons in my life so I can be prepared for everything that is coming next. In Jesus's name, amen.

for the record

THESE ARE THE MOMENTS I DON'T WANT TO FORGET

give thanks
in all circumstances

3 THINGS I'M THANKFUL FOR TODAY

1

2

3

my story

Have you ever heard someone ask why God doesn't do something about all the hunger or poverty around the world? Sometimes I think we forget that God cares more about people than we do, and maybe that reality is the problem. He wants us to care about His people as much as He does. He wants us to be His hands and feet. So how do we know what needs God is calling us to meet? They say if you find something that breaks your heart, you can be sure it breaks God's heart as well.

BASED ON THE THINGS THAT CAUSE YOUR HEART TO BREAK, WHAT NEEDS DO YOU THINK GOD MIGHT BE CALLING YOU TO MEET IN THIS SEASON?

to be honest ...

THIS IS HOW I REALLY FEEL TODAY

Lord, when I see so much pain and sadness in the world, I can trust that You see it too. You saw it first. Help me become part of the solution. Help me see the needs that I have the capacity to meet right now. Forgive me for being consumed with what is going on in my own life when You have asked me to be Your hands and feet, caring for the world around me and carrying Your love everywhere I go. Show me what I can do today to influence those around me with Your love. In Jesus's name, amen.

for the record

THESE ARE THE MOMENTS I DON'T WANT TO FORGET

give thanks
in all circumstances

3 THINGS I'M THANKFUL FOR TODAY

1

2

3

my story

When my kids were little and the house was always noisy, I would retreat to my back porch in the evenings after my husband came home from work. It was so peaceful, and I often just needed a minute away from all the demands of the day. Life has changed, and even though my children are growing up, peace and quiet are still hard to find. I look for peace in new places now, and I find it by sipping my coffee a little more slowly or playing a worship song during an otherwise stressful car ride. I have taught my heart how to find peace even when there is no quiet.

WHERE DO YOU FIND PEACE PRESENTLY?

to be honest ...

THIS IS HOW I REALLY FEEL TODAY

Lord, in Your Word You told Your disciples, "Peace I leave with you; my peace I give you .... Do not let your hearts be troubled and do not be afraid" (John 14:27). I know that peace is a gift You give freely. Help me take hold of this gift and rest in it this week. Help me find the places where Your peace can transcend my circumstances and shift my environment. In Jesus's name, amen.

for the record

THESE ARE THE MOMENTS I DON'T WANT TO FORGET

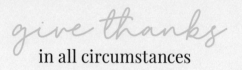

in all circumstances

———

3 THINGS I'M THANKFUL FOR TODAY

1

2

3

my story

Have you ever experienced a quiet season when the Lord didn't seem to do much talking and you weren't even certain He was there? While there are times when we can see God working on our behalf and feel confident in His continued presence, there are other times when He just seems distant. Despite how we feel, we can trust that the Lord never leaves us. When God said He would send His Holy Spirit to be with us, it was a promise for every moment of our lives. He is always with us and for us.

<<<<<

HOW CAN YOU BE CERTAIN THAT GOD
IS WITH YOU IN THIS SEASON?

>>>>>

to be honest...

THIS IS HOW I REALLY FEEL TODAY

Lord, I want to be sure of Your presence. I want to be confident that You are with me. Your Word says You never leave me and never forsake me, but sometimes that is hard to believe. Help me know deep within my heart that You are with me right here, right now. Soften my heart to be sensitive to the presence of Your Holy Spirit. Raise my level of expectation to feel You near me and to hear Your voice reminding me of Your closeness. In Jesus's name, amen.

for the record

THESE ARE THE MOMENTS I DON'T WANT TO FORGET

give thanks
in all circumstances

3 THINGS I'M THANKFUL FOR TODAY

1

2

3

my story

When God made Adam and placed him in the garden, He gave him everything he needed—food, a relationship with Him, assignments to complete. However, Adam didn't have a helper, and God said it wasn't good for man to be alone. So God made woman (Genesis 2:7–23). God shows us throughout Scripture that it still isn't good for us to be alone. God's kingdom grows when we are in community, spurring one another on in our faith and sharing His love with the world. Community can shift and change throughout life, but it is important that we stay connected to one another.

WHAT DOES COMMUNITY LOOK LIKE RIGHT NOW IN YOUR LIFE?

to be honest...

THIS IS HOW I REALLY FEEL TODAY

Lord, thank You for knitting my heart together with others who are following You. You bring people into my life who love to be in Your presence and are on a similar journey to know You better. Thank You for my family and friends both near and far, God. Thank You for each person who currently makes up my community. In Jesus's name, amen.

for the record

THESE ARE THE MOMENTS I DON'T WANT TO FORGET

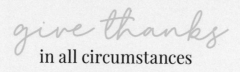

give thanks
in all circumstances

3 THINGS I'M THANKFUL FOR TODAY

1

2

3

my story

Every fear the Enemy whispers to our hearts is an assault against God's character. When we are afraid we are going to run out of money, it is an affront to God our provider. When we are afraid we have to do it all on our own, the Enemy wants us to believe that God is not our helper. If we can identify our fear, then we can know exactly how to pray.

‹‹‹‹‹

WHERE IS FEAR THE LOUDEST IN YOUR
LIFE RIGHT NOW? COMPLETE THIS SENTENCE:
"GOD, I KNOW YOU'RE _____.
I BELIEVE YOU ARE WHO YOU SAY YOU ARE."

›››››

to be honest...

THIS IS HOW I REALLY FEEL TODAY

Lord, thank You for foiling the plans of the Enemy. In each circumstance where the Enemy wants me to cower in fear, You have already won the battle. There is no reason to be afraid. There is no reason to retreat. I believe You are who You say You are. You are good. You are my provider. You are my helper. You are my strength. You are everything I need. In Jesus's name, amen.

for the record

THESE ARE THE MOMENTS I DON'T WANT TO FORGET

give thanks
in all circumstances

3 THINGS I'M THANKFUL FOR TODAY

1

2

3

my story

I have to admit that when life feels hard or I'm facing a particularly trying situation, I don't always pray first. I often worry, call a friend to fret over the phone, or avoid the situation altogether. However, Scripture reminds us that we have been given tools to help us persevere in even the most difficult times. We have the Bible, we have community, and we have the Holy Spirit.

WHEN YOU ARE FACED WITH A
CHALLENGING SITUATION OR CRISIS,
WHAT ARE THE FIRST STEPS YOU TAKE?

to be honest...

THIS IS HOW I REALLY FEEL TODAY

Lord, You invite me to bring all my petitions to You. Through Jesus, You made a way for me to lay all my burdens at Your feet. You sent Your Son so I could find my way back to You and have complete access to Your heart and Your wisdom. However, oftentimes I don't bring my needs to You. Instead, I try to deal with them on my own. Remind me of the power of prayer. In Jesus's name, amen.

for the record

THESE ARE THE MOMENTS I DON'T WANT TO FORGET

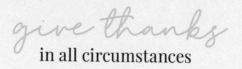

in all circumstances

3 THINGS I'M THANKFUL FOR TODAY

1

2

3

my story

One of the most unusual places I have ever been when I heard God speak to my heart was driving in my minivan with a back seat full of noisy kids. I used to think the Lord would speak only when I had my Bible open and was completely silent. But as I have read Scripture, I have discovered that the Lord breaks into the ordinary lives of His people in unusual ways to deliver messages from His heart. Though I can always hear His heart when I read His Word, sometimes He speaks through dreams or through the words of a wise friend.

❮❮❮❮❮

FILL IN THIS BLANK:
I OFTEN FIND THAT THE LORD SPEAKS TO ME

_____.

❯❯❯❯❯

to be honest …

THIS IS HOW I REALLY FEEL TODAY

Lord, I want You to lead me. I want to know for certain that the direction I am heading is in line with the steps You'd have me take. I don't want to make one move forward without You as my guide. Help me tune in to Your voice this week so I can be confident You are leading me. In Jesus's name, amen.

for the record

THESE ARE THE MOMENTS I DON'T WANT TO FORGET

give thanks
in all circumstances

3 THINGS I'M THANKFUL FOR TODAY

1

2

3

my story

I don't have much margin in my schedule for moments of rest. From the time I wake up until the time I go to sleep, there are things to do—and not many of them are on my list of favorite tasks to accomplish. Even the small breaks I do get are consumed with swirling thoughts of what I need to get done. My heart craves the chance to pause and breathe with the Father. Throughout our lives, rest looks different depending on the season we are in.

HOW ARE YOU CURRENTLY PURSUING REST?

to be honest ...

THIS IS HOW I REALLY FEEL TODAY

Lord, even when my schedule is full and my heart feels rushed, show me places where I can rest. Remind my heart of the importance of pausing in Your presence. I don't want to feel as though I cannot take a breath. I want to lean back into Your love and feel Your heartbeat carrying the rhythm of rest. Help me find moments of peace with You. In Jesus's name, amen.

for the record

THESE ARE THE MOMENTS I DON'T WANT TO FORGET

give thanks
in all circumstances

---

3 THINGS I'M THANKFUL FOR TODAY

1

2

3

my story

When I read the story in Mark 4 about the sudden storm that didn't just rock the disciples in their boat but rocked them to the core, I imagine the size of the waves. I imagine the salty air, the rain, and how hard it must have been to stand on their ship. I think of how violent this storm must have been, and when I picture the Lord declaring "Peace!" I recognize how shocking the stillness must have been in contrast to the raging waters. The Lord wants to declare peace with such boldness that sudden stillness settles over our hearts as well.

IN WHAT AREA OF YOUR LIFE DO YOU NEED THE LORD TO DECLARE PEACE?

to be honest ...

THIS IS HOW I REALLY FEEL TODAY

Lord, there are so many times when I feel as though I'm on a ship being tossed by the waves. My emotions, my relationships, and my schedule so often feel full of hurry and chaos. God, I ask that You would declare peace over my heart. Settle every area of turmoil. Remind me that I have the ability to speak to the wind and waves the Enemy uses to knock me from my footing. In Jesus's name, amen.

for the record

THESE ARE THE MOMENTS I DON'T WANT TO FORGET

give thanks
in all circumstances

3 THINGS I'M THANKFUL FOR TODAY

1

2

3

my story

___

Y ou're just going to mess up again. That nasty little thought creeps into my mind when I have not handled a situation with my family or friends in the best way. Guilt tells me I'm not doing my best and tries to convince me something is wrong with me. I believe that guilt is one of the Enemy's favorite tools to use against us. Guilt keeps us trapped so we are unable to move forward and accept God's full forgiveness. I have come to realize that conviction from the Holy Spirit teaches us how to correct our mistakes, while condemnation from the Enemy tells us we *are* the mistake.

‹‹‹‹‹

IN WHAT AREA OF YOUR LIFE IS GUILT
TRYING TO STEAL YOUR CONFIDENCE?

›››››

to be honest ...

THIS IS HOW I REALLY FEEL TODAY

Lord, I don't want to spend my days buried under the burden of shame. I don't want to feel as though I am constantly not quite measuring up. Show me how to receive Your grace, God. Show me how to start again even when I make mistakes. Forgiveness isn't permission to fail again; it's simply a fresh start that frees me from the fear of failure. Thank You for Your continuous forgiveness, God. In Jesus's name, amen.

for the record

THESE ARE THE MOMENTS I DON'T WANT TO FORGET

give thanks
in all circumstances

3 THINGS I'M THANKFUL FOR TODAY

1

2

3

my story

Sometimes when my husband is in the other room and I want to ask him a question, I just shout. "Hey, honey! What did you do with that paper that was on my desk?" If he doesn't answer right away, I yell again. "Can you hear me?" Pause. "Are you ignoring me?" There's usually a good reason why my husband doesn't answer. More than once I've gone into the other room after shouting and found him in the middle of an important phone call. In the same way, sometimes we become frustrated when the Lord doesn't answer us immediately, even though He always has a good reason.

HOW DO YOU RESPOND WHEN GOD'S
ANSWERS ARE DELAYED?

to be honest ...

THIS IS HOW I REALLY FEEL TODAY

Lord, sometimes in my impatience I begin to question Your character. I wonder why You aren't moving as quickly as I'd hoped You would. I wonder what You're doing when You're silent or the answers seem delayed. Help me remember that You don't hide Yourself from me. Instead, You sent the Holy Spirit to be with me so I would know that even when the answers take longer than I'd like, You have not left me. Give me patience in the waiting. In Jesus's name, amen.

for the record

THESE ARE THE MOMENTS I DON'T WANT TO FORGET

give thanks

in all circumstances

3 THINGS I'M THANKFUL FOR TODAY

DATE

1

2

3

my story

W hen I was growing up, there was an expression in church that was repeated frequently. One person would say, "God is good." Someone else would reply, "All the time." Then the first person would say, "And all the time," and the other person would respond, "God is good." It's kind of cheesy, but it helped me learn from a young age that God and goodness go together. Today I understand that God's goodness is a key part of His character. We must trust that He is good in order to trust in His love.

<<<<<

WHEN YOU THINK OF GOD'S GOODNESS, WHAT COMES TO MIND?

>>>>>

to be honest ...

THIS IS HOW I REALLY FEEL TODAY

Lord, even in the hardest times, Your goodness remains true. Psalm 136:1 says, "Give thanks to the LORD, for he is good. His love endures forever." I can see Your goodness revealed in Your mercy. Thank You for every merciful gift. Thank You for sparing me from every attack of the Enemy, even when I haven't been aware of it. Thank You for mercifully giving me what I need rather than what I want. In Jesus's name, amen.

for the record

THESE ARE THE MOMENTS I DON'T WANT TO FORGET

give thanks

in all circumstances

3 THINGS I'M THANKFUL FOR TODAY

DATE

1

2

3

my story

"I'm stuck!" The call came from my son's room. My three-year-old had pulled most of his toys from their buckets and had surrounded himself with a mound of all his favorite things. He'd enjoyed playing with them until he realized that in order to get to the door, he'd have to either put the toys away or be lifted over them. He wasn't hurt. He wasn't trapped forever, but the task of putting everything away seemed overwhelming. However, he knew who would come for him. He knew how to ask for help.

≪≪≪≪

FROM WHAT OVERWHELMING SITUATION
DO YOU NEED THE LORD TO FREE YOU?

≫≫≫≫

to be honest…

THIS IS HOW I REALLY FEEL TODAY

Lord, sometimes I find myself in situations that seem absolutely overwhelming. I can't see a clear way out of them, and the task of cleaning them up and making my way to the other side seems impossible. In those moments, thank You for not telling me, "Well, you got yourself in there. You can get yourself out." No, instead You simply come to my rescue, freeing me from everything the Enemy uses to trap me. Remind me that I can always call for help. In Jesus's name, amen.

for the record

THESE ARE THE MOMENTS I DON'T WANT TO FORGET

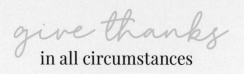
give thanks
in all circumstances

3 THINGS I'M THANKFUL FOR TODAY

1

2

3

my story

I've experienced times in my life when laughter didn't bubble up easily. Stress or busyness distracted my heart. Anxiety stole my ability to truly enjoy my life, my family, and my friends. I've had other times when it was easier to find joy in the middle of the ordinary moments. Sometimes we have to fight for joy. We have to fight to move from a place of anxiety or busyness or routine so that we can have the strength joy provides. Nehemiah 8:10 reminds us, "The joy of the LORD is your strength."

≪≪≪≪

WHERE DO YOU FIND JOY PRESENTLY?

≫≫≫≫

to be honest...

THIS IS HOW I REALLY FEEL TODAY

Lord, when I first fell in love with You, I felt so happy and free. Today I pray that the joy I first experienced when I agreed to follow You would flood my heart. Scripture makes it clear that my heart produces joy when I'm in a close relationship with You. When joy seems lost, help me find it in Your presence, God. In Jesus's name, amen.

for the record

THESE ARE THE MOMENTS I DON'T WANT TO FORGET

give thanks

in all circumstances

3 THINGS I'M THANKFUL FOR TODAY

1

2

3

my story

When I got married, one of the first questions I was asked was, "When are you going to have kids?" After I had my first child, it wasn't long before people started asking my husband and me if we were thinking of having another. It seems it is easy for others to look toward the future and see the next logical step in our lives, but only the Lord knows what He has planned for us in His heart. Sometimes His plans don't seem logical and don't align with the expectations of others. But as you look toward the future, dream for just a moment.

WHAT DO YOU THINK GOD IS
CALLING YOU TO NEXT?

to be honest ...

THIS IS HOW I REALLY FEEL TODAY

Lord, give me Your dreams. Place within me a desire for more—not more stuff or more fame or more money but more of You and everything You have in store for my life. Show me what You're calling me to next so that I can dream with You. In Jesus's name, amen.

DATE

for the record

THESE ARE THE MOMENTS I DON'T WANT TO FORGET

give thanks
in all circumstances

---

3 THINGS I'M THANKFUL FOR TODAY

1

2

3

my story

Google has a lot of great information that answers just about any question we might have. But Google can't tell us what God has planned for us. If we're going to discover exactly what the Lord wants us to do, we have to consult a far better resource. We have to find wise counsel, spend time in the Word, and actively seek the wisdom of the Holy Spirit.

WHAT PRACTICAL STEPS ARE YOU TAKING
TO FIND WISDOM, PEACE, AND GOD'S
HEART FOR THE JOURNEY AHEAD?

to be honest ...

THIS IS HOW I REALLY FEEL TODAY

Lord, Your Word says in John 14:26 that Your Holy Spirit will teach me. Thank You for showing me which doors to walk through next. I ask that You'd bring people into my life who can speak peace to my questioning heart. Guide me as only You can, God. As I actively seek Your wisdom, I thank You for not withholding Your counsel. In Jesus's name, amen.

DATE

for the record

THESE ARE THE MOMENTS I DON'T WANT TO FORGET

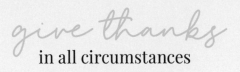

give thanks
in all circumstances

3 THINGS I'M THANKFUL FOR TODAY

1

2

3

my story

We live in a time when we can have groceries, fast food, and online purchases delivered to our homes within hours. We can instantly download movies and songs and applications to make our lives easier. There isn't much we have to wait for anymore. However, the kingdom of God operates on the principle of seedtime and harvest, and Scripture reminds us to work toward the seasons to come. While it would be wonderful if we saw immediate results when we sow into the lives of others, many times we invest and then wait years to see a harvest.

WHAT SEEDS ARE YOU PLANTING TODAY THAT YOU HOPE TO HARVEST IN THE FUTURE?

to be honest...

THIS IS HOW I REALLY FEEL TODAY

Lord, help me remember the importance of pouring into the lives of those around me. Even in the ordinary parts of my day, remind me that I am sowing into eternity. I am planting seeds of love that will grow and lead others to You. God, even when I wish I could see the immediate results of my love and prayers, grow patience within me as I remember that You will receive glory as I continue to invest in Your kingdom. In Jesus's name, amen.

for the record

THESE ARE THE MOMENTS I DON'T WANT TO FORGET

give thanks
in all circumstances

---

3 THINGS I'M THANKFUL FOR TODAY

1

2

3

my story

Before I met my husband, I spent much of my time praying for him. I wondered where he was and what he was doing. I prayed for our life together and for our children. I prayed for the work God would call us to take on together. I did a lot of praying forward in that season, but that hasn't always been the case. I've had times, too, when I've focused too much on what was happening around me and paid very little attention to what would come next. In spite of this, the next season always comes.

DESCRIBE YOUR PRAYER STRATEGY
FOR THE SEASON AHEAD.

to be honest...

THIS IS HOW I REALLY FEEL TODAY

Lord, as I look ahead, I trust that You have already gone before me, making a way for me to transition into the next phase of life. Because You know what's coming, I ask that You will teach me what to pray. Give me words to pray that agree with what's in Your heart so that Your will may be accomplished in my life. In Jesus's name, amen.

for the record

THESE ARE THE MOMENTS I DON'T WANT TO FORGET

give thanks
in all circumstances

3 THINGS I'M THANKFUL FOR TODAY

1

2

3

my story

I drove down our old street and came to a stop in front of our previous home. When we lived there, so many aspects of my life seemed hard. I often felt overwhelmed and exhausted as a mom of three small children. But as I looked back on those difficult moments, I thought about when I pulled my babies in a wagon around the block and when they ran through the sprinklers in their diapers. No matter how trying the times are, the sweet moments pass alongside the hard ones.

WHAT DO YOU THINK YOU WILL MISS MOST WHEN THIS SEASON IS OVER?

to be honest...

THIS IS HOW I REALLY FEEL TODAY

Lord, when I think of what comes next, it's often partially because I am so eager to leave my current challenges behind. I long to slip into an ease that I imagine is waiting for me in the future. So I pause right now to acknowledge the gifts and joys I currently possess. I take a quick inventory of the blessings in my life, knowing that tomorrow's blessings might come in a different package. Thank You for being the Father who sends good gifts in each season of life. In Jesus's name, amen.

for the record

DATE

THESE ARE THE MOMENTS I DON'T WANT TO FORGET

give thanks
in all circumstances

3 THINGS I'M THANKFUL FOR TODAY

1

2

3

my story

Have you ever been through something challenging and wondered what God was trying to teach you? Maybe you experienced a delay in receiving an answer to your prayers and wondered if God was trying to develop your patience. Maybe God asked you to follow Him in a direction that didn't make sense from your perspective, and it felt as though He was trying to teach you how to trust Him. We can be confident that in every season, we will have opportunities to discover God's character and love for us in a new way.

≪≪≪≪

WHAT DO YOU THINK GOD WANTS YOU TO
LEARN ABOUT HIM THROUGH THE SITUATIONS
YOU'RE CURRENTLY FACING?

≫≫≫≫

to be honest ...

THIS IS HOW I REALLY FEEL TODAY

Lord, though You never change, I continually discover more about You as You reveal new aspects of Your heart to me. As I learn who You are, I more fully understand who I am in You. Teach me what You want me to learn about Your character so I can be a better representation of Your heart and nature to the world around me. In Jesus's name, amen.

for the record

THESE ARE THE MOMENTS I DON'T WANT TO FORGET

give thanks
in all circumstances

---

3 THINGS I'M THANKFUL FOR TODAY

1

2

3

my story

I once had a friend who used to pray, *Lord, help me learn the lesson of this season quickly so I can move on to the next.* This was her prayer particularly in trying times because she knew that the Lord wanted her to learn from her situation, and she wanted to be a quicker learner. She understood that the Lord sometimes uses certain circumstances to teach us and shape our character, but she wasn't always a fan of how He taught her. We can be confident that God doesn't waste one moment in teaching our hearts and building us up.

❬❬❬❬❬

WHAT HAS BEEN THE LESSON IN THIS SEASON OF YOUR LIFE?

❭❭❭❭❭

to be honest...

THIS IS HOW I REALLY FEEL TODAY

Lord, I pray that You'd help me learn completely the lessons You currently want to teach me. Thank You for instructing my heart and for shaping my character. Thank You for the wisdom I will acquire in this season that will prepare me for the next. I don't want to rush past the insight I am gaining here that will be necessary in the days ahead. Help me become a patient and eager student of Your love. In Jesus's name, amen.

for the record

THESE ARE THE MOMENTS I DON'T WANT TO FORGET

give thanks
in all circumstances
_____

3 THINGS I'M THANKFUL FOR TODAY

1

2

3

my story

There is a story in Luke 18:35–43 about a blind man who heard that Jesus was passing by and began calling to Him. Jesus had this man brought to Him, and He asked him, "What do you want me to do for you?" The man answered, "I want to see." Even though the Lord knew everything about this man, including the fact that he was blind, Jesus still asked him what he wanted. He does the same for us. Even though God knows our needs, He still gives us the opportunity to ask Him for help.

WHAT DO YOU NEED THE LORD TO HELP YOU WITH THIS WEEK?

DATE _____

to be honest...

THIS IS HOW I REALLY FEEL TODAY

Lord, I am so grateful that I can come to You for help any-time. I don't have to wait my turn or hope You have a free moment to spend with me. You sent Your Holy Spirit so I can constantly be in Your presence and have access to You al-ways. Thank You for being the God who meets every need in my life. In Jesus's name, amen.

for the record

THESE ARE THE MOMENTS I DON'T WANT TO FORGET

give thanks
in all circumstances

---

3 THINGS I'M THANKFUL FOR TODAY

1

2

3

my story

My husband and I lost our first two babies to miscarriage. Both losses were devastating times in our lives. We were in so much pain and had many questions. But as the Lord led us kindly through the process of healing, our hope returned, and I knew what I needed to do. I needed to encourage other women who were still in deep heartache after suffering their own losses. I needed to help guide those who were still processing their grief. I believe there are people who will find hope in your story too. Think about the ways your unique experiences could help or encourage people you know.

IS THERE SOMEONE IN NEED OF SUPPORT WHOM YOU CAN INSPIRE, HELP, OR ENCOURAGE?

to be honest ...

THIS IS HOW I REALLY FEEL TODAY

Lord, when I am in the middle of the trial or the heartache or the confusion, it's nearly impossible to see what good is going to come from it. But I believe that You can use every part of my journey to lead others to a place of healing and wholeness. I give You permission to use my story, and I ask that You'd send me into the lives of others who need Your hope and healing. In Jesus's name, amen.

for the record

THESE ARE THE MOMENTS I DON'T WANT TO FORGET

give thanks
in all circumstances

3 THINGS I'M THANKFUL FOR TODAY

1

2

3

About the Author

Born and raised in Oklahoma, Becky Thompson is a transplant to Los Angeles, where she lives with her husband, Jared, and their three children. She is the author of the books *Hope Unfolding, Love Unending*, and *Truth Unchanging*, writing about the often overlooked struggle of balancing life as a wife, mother, and daughter of God. Becky's passion is to see the hearts of her readers revived by God's love so they can better know Him and make Him better known. Listen to Becky weekly on the *Revived Motherhood* podcast or connect online at BeckyThompson.com.